Bottle-Nosed Dolphins

A Buddy Book
by
Julie Murray

VISIT US AT
www.abdopub.com

Published by Buddy Books, an imprint of ABDO Publishing Company, 4940 Viking Drive, Suite 622, Edina, Minnesota 55435. Copyright © 2005 by Abdo Consulting Group, Inc. International copyrights reserved in all countries. No part of this book may be reproduced in any form without written permission from the publisher.

Printed in the United States.

Edited by: Christy DeVillier
Contributing Editors: Matt Ray, Michael P. Goecke
Graphic Design: Maria Hosley
Image Research: Deborah Coldiron
Photographs: Corbis, Corel, Digital Vision, Minden Pictures, Photodisc, Yesterdays

Library of Congress Cataloging-in-Publication Data

Murray, Julie, 1969-
   Bottle-nosed dolphins / Julie Murray.
      p. cm. — (Animal kingdom)
   Includes bibliographical references (p.) and index.
   Contents: Dolphins — Bottle-nosed dolphins — What they look like — Where they live — What they eat — Breathing — Senses — Groups — Babies.
   ISBN 1-59197-304-X
      1. Bottle-nosed dolphin—Juvenile literature. [1. Bottle-nosed dolphin. 2. Dolphins.] I. Title.

QL737.C432M856 2003
599.53'3—dc22

                                                                2003056269

Contents

Dolphins

There are 37 kinds of dolphins. They live in oceans and rivers around the world. Dolphins are very playful. They often leap out of the water. Dolphins sometimes swim alongside boats, too.

Dolphins, whales, and porpoises live in water. But these animals are not fish. They are sea mammals. Walruses, sea lions, and seals are sea mammals, too.

Dolphins are sea mammals.

Mammals use lungs to breathe air. They are born alive instead of hatching from eggs. Baby mammals drink their mother's milk. Giraffes, pigs, hamsters, and people are mammals, too.

Most mammals have hair to keep them warm. Adult dolphins do not have hair. A thick layer of fat under their skin keeps them warm. This fat is called blubber.

Giraffes and pigs are
mammals that live on land.

Bottle-Nosed Dolphins

Bottle-nosed dolphins are playful, curious, and friendly to people. They are named after the shape of their nose, or beak. The shape of their mouth makes people think they are smiling.

Bottle-nosed dolphins look like they are smiling.

Bottle-nosed dolphins live in large groups called herds. Some herds have as many as 1,000 members. There are smaller groups within the herd. These smaller groups are called pods.

Bottle-nosed dolphins enjoy living with each other.

Living in groups helps bottle-nosed dolphins guard against predators. Some predators of dolphins are killer whales and sharks.

Sharks and killer whales hunt bottle-nosed dolphins.

Performing Dolphins

Scientists believe dolphins are some of the smartest animals. Bottle-nosed dolphins can follow commands and learn tricks. They can jump through hoops and throw balls through nets. Many people enjoy watching bottle-nosed dolphins perform at zoos and aquariums.

What They Look Like

Most bottle-nosed dolphins grow to become about nine feet (three m) long. Some adults are as long as 13 feet (four m). Most bottle-nosed dolphins weigh between 400 and 600 pounds (181 and 272 kg). Males are commonly larger than females.

Bottle-nosed dolphins are long and sleek. They have a gray back and a white or pinkish gray belly. Flippers help dolphins stay balanced as they swim. Dolphins also have strong fins on their tail. These fins, or flukes, help them swim fast.

Bottle-nosed dolphins can swim as fast as 25 miles (40 km) per hour.

All dolphins have a blowhole for taking in air. This blowhole is on top of the dolphin's head. Dolphins shut their blowhole before going under water. They can stay under water for many minutes.

Dolphins take in air through their blowhole.

Where They Live

Bottle-nosed dolphins live in warm waters around the world. They live as far north as Japan and Norway. They live as far south as Argentina and New Zealand. Bottle-nosed dolphins live near the southern tip of Africa, too.

Some dolphins migrate every year.

Some bottle-nosed dolphins stay in one area their whole lives. Others migrate during the year. Bottle-nosed dolphins often go wherever their food goes. Sometimes they travel to warmer waters when the seasons change.

Eating

Bottle-nosed dolphins only eat meat. They eat small fish, squid, eels, crabs, lobsters, and octopuses. Bottle-nosed dolphins can eat as much as 30 pounds (14 kg) of food each day.

Sometimes, a pod of dolphins works together to trap fish. They will swim underneath and around a group of fish. This makes it easier for the pod to catch the fish.

Bottle-nosed dolphins have more than 100 sharp teeth. They use their teeth to catch fish. Bottle-nosed dolphins do not chew their food. They swallow it whole.

Bottle-nosed dolphins have many sharp teeth.

Dolphin Sounds

 Bottle-nosed dolphins communicate with each other. They do this through touch, movements, and sounds. Dolphins make whistles, clicks, and chirps. Nobody fully understands what these sounds mean.

Dolphins use sounds to find food, too. They will make sounds, then listen to the echoes. The echoes tell them the size and shape of what is ahead. This is called echolocation.

Scientists study dolphins to understand how they communicate.

Dolphin Calves

Dolphin babies are called calves. Female bottle-nosed dolphins have one baby at a time. Calves are born under water. Newborn calves are more than three feet (one m) long. They weigh as much as 40 pounds (18 kg).

The mother helps a newborn calf swim to the surface for air. The calf stays close to her and drinks her milk. After about four months, the calf begins eating fish.

Calves stay with their mothers for about three years. Bottle-nosed dolphins can live to be 35 years old.

Important Words

aquarium a building that keeps fish and water animals for display.

blowhole the opening on top of a dolphin's head used for taking in air.

communicate to give and receive information. Talking is one way people communicate.

echolocation using sounds and echoes to learn the shape and size of objects ahead.

flippers the flat, paddle-shaped body parts that dolphins use to swim.

mammal most living things that belong to this special group have hair, give birth to live babies, and make milk to feed their babies.

migrate to move from one place to another when the seasons change.

predator an animal that hunts and eats other animals.

Web Sites

To learn more about bottle-nosed dolphins, visit ABDO Publishing Company on the World Wide Web. Web sites about bottle-nosed dolphins are featured on our Book Links page. These links are routinely monitored and updated to provide the most current information available.

www.abdopub.com

Index